Forty
Favourite Things

*A compilation of poems, scriptures,
prayers, inspirational quotes plus much more*

Olubukolami Adebayo

AuthorHouse™ UK
1663 Liberty Drive
Bloomington, IN 47403 USA
www.authorhouse.co.uk
UK TFN: 0800 0148641 (Toll Free inside the UK)
UK Local: 02036 956322 (+44 20 3695 6322 from outside the UK)

This book is printed on acid-free paper.

ISBN: 978-1-6655-9110-2 (sc)
ISBN: 978-1-6655-9111-9 (e)

Print information available on the last page.

Published by AuthorHouse 06/26/2021

authorHOUSE®

I am so delighted to share a part of my life with you as God has kept me thus far in His Faithfulness. To God be all the Glory.

Olubukolami Tolulope Adebayo

Here are 40 of my favourite things…

10 Favourite Scriptures (NKJV) and Declarations

1. The lines have fallen to me in pleasant places; Yes, I have a good inheritance. *(Psalms 16:6)*

   Declaration - I have a good and desirable heritage…because the Almighty God is my portion, I have favour, mercy, grace and divine blessings. I shall not lack anything good.

2. I have set the Lord always before me; Because He is at my right hand I shall not be moved. *(Psalms 16:8)*

   Declaration - I am divinely protected, the Lord is at my right hand, He shields me, He is my refuge, strength and fortress.

3. The thief does not come except to steal, and to kill, and to destroy. I have come that they may have life, and that they may have it more abundantly. *(John 10:10)*

   Declaration - I have total victory over the enemy by the Power of the Most High, I have a beautiful life through Jesus my Lord.

4. Oh, taste and see that the Lord is good; Blessed is the man who trusts in Him! *(Psalms 34:8)*

   Declaration - Because I trust in the Lord, blessings, goodness and the beauty of the Lord are forever my portion.

5. "The Lord bless you and keep you; The Lord make His face shine upon you and be gracious to you, the Lord lift up His countenance upon you, And give you peace." *(Numbers 6:24 - 26)*

   Declaration - The Lord will continually bless me, lead me in the way of righteousness, protect me from all harm, grant me favour in all I do and give me peace in all situations.

6. The Lord will perfect that which concerns me; Your mercy, O Lord, endures forever; Do not forsake the works of Your hands. *(Psalms 138:8)*

   Declaration - God will accomplish all that concerns me and establish the works of my hands. All things are working for my good, God is mindful of me, He will prosper the works of my hands, He will never reject or abandon me. He is always reliable so I trust Him to always come through for me.

7. And we know that all things work together for good to those who love God, to those who are called according to His purpose. *(Romans 8:28)*

Declaration - Because I am God's elect, His favourite daughter, everything I go through in life will have a Positive outcome because God's plans for me are always Good and not evil to give me an expected end. I will fulfil God's plan and purpose for my life.

8. And Jabez called on the God of Israel saying, "Oh, that You would bless me indeed, and enlarge my territory, that Your hand would be with me, and that You would keep me from evil, that I may not cause pain!" So God granted him what he requested. *(I Chronicles 4:10)*

Declaration - I am Blessed of the Lord, every unpleasant situation in my life is turning around and working in my favour, I am beautiful, strong, favoured and divinely covered. My disappointments are turning into Glorious appointments. I am compensated for all my labour.

9. Trust in the Lord with all your heart, And lean not on your own understanding; In all your ways acknowledge Him, And He shall direct your path. *(Proverbs 3:5 - 6)*

Declaration - Because I put my trust in you Lord Jesus, I have a clear path, I have knowledge, wisdom and understanding, I have direction because you lead and guide me in all my ways.

10. Finally, brethren, whatever things are true, whatever things are noble, whatever things are just, whatever things are pure, whatever things are lovely, whatever things are of good report, if there is any virtue and if there is anything praiseworthy— meditate on these things. *(Philippians 4: 8)*

Declaration - I have a relationship with my Lord and master Jesus Christ because of this, my eyes and heart are fixed and steadfast, all that flows from me is sweet, beautiful and admirable. My thoughts are pure, I dwell only on things that are true, honest, just, pure, lovely and of good report.

Olubukolami's Favourite Snack and Dessert

11.   **Snack** - Popcorn

    Dessert- Vanilla Ice cream and fruit bowl

Olubukolami's Hobbies

12.   Music & Movies, Baking, travelling to fun places, reading and spending quality time with family and friends.

Olubukolami's Best
attributes and Core values

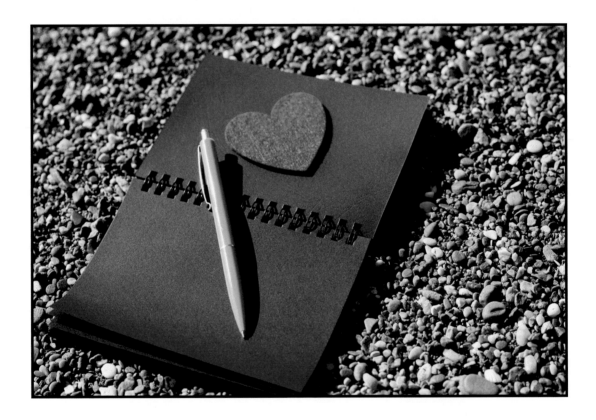

13. **Best attributes** - Generous, down to earth, eye for detail, loves to plan and organise, great administrator.

Core Values - Honesty and integrity, Compassion, Hardwork and Loyalty.

Olubukolami's 7 **Favourite**
Hymns and what it means to her…

14.   To God be the Glory, great things He has done - Fanny Crosby

*God is forever faithful, I will praise His name. He knows my end from the beginning and has my life planned for great things. To Him be all the Glory

15. Be Glad in the Lord and Rejoice - Mary Servoss

*It is great to thank God, always. Be Glad and thankful through the good and the bad. Your testimony is sure.

16. There shall be showers of Blessing - Daniel Webster

*God's blessings know no bounds. It flows abundantly, He daily loads us with benefits.

17. Deeper Deeper in the Love of Jesus - Charles Price Jones

*Daily working and walking with God, yearning to know Him more and more. Growing deeper in His word and in His Love

18. Great is thy Faithfulness, Oh God my Father - Thomas Chisholm

*God's Faithfulness and love is unwavering. His mercies are new every morning.

19. Have you been to Jesus for the cleansing Power - Elisha Hoffman

*The cleansing Power of the Blood of Jesus makes us pure and white as snow, qualifying us to have a relationship with our Father in Heaven.

20. What a Friend we have in Jesus - Joseph M Scriven

*Jesus is the friend that sticks closer than a brother, he never leaves or forsake us even when everyone does, He is dependable and reliable, the ever present help in time of need.

Olubukolami's Favourite
Phrases (and why I say these…)

21.   'Do you understand?'

Communication is a two way street, whenever I speak to people I check in frequently to make sure they are being carried along, listening actively and still with me. I love a two way engagement…so I have been told severally I use this phrase… LOL

'God have mercy!'

Well, I don't know how I picked this up but I know it is only by God's grace and mercy I am where I am today and still standing…

Olubukolami's Favourite Foods

22.   Porridge (oats), Rice dishes + Plantain

Olubukolami's Favourite Clothing Style

23.   T shirts + Jeans + Trainers /pumps/flats (I simply love comfort)

24.   For Dad (Of Blessed memory)

A dad is someone who cares,
Someone to count on,
Someone whose shoulder you lean on,
A Rock, so strong, so true
Someone to trust, one whose courage inspires,
Someone who stands Solid...immovable
Someone to look up to
A priest of His home in every sense of the word...
One with dignity and integrity
One with conviction, self respect and pride
One whose legacy never dies
I love you Dad.

25.   My Mummy dearest (Iyaest)

You are a woman of such Grace
Your journey has not been easy
But your faith has never faltered
and your heart so pure, you Love God
You love family, you love others

A woman of great humility, patience and strength
A woman with such great words of wisdom
A queen that paves the way for others…
A true Proverbs 31 woman
I love and admire you
My very own sweet mum

26.   LOVE (Provides the answer)

To every new door
Love provides the Key to open it

To every new hurdle
A companion to help you over it

For every burden
Support to bear it

For all of life's questions
For all hassles, unrest and pain
A God to share, bear and heal

For all of life's questions
Love provides the answer

27.   JC (Jesus Christ)

Your Love for me is incomparable
Your Grace for me is inestimable
You are hope, joy and life to me
You have been near me through thick and thin
I can Boldly say
You are my all in all
Simply because
I can call on you on all situations

You can be sure of one thing JC
You have my heart and you always will
You know me through and through
You first loved me

And for this,
I will always be there
To talk about you
To talk to you

I appreciate you Lord
For all you have done and
For things you're yet to do

28.   Sisters (F, B & S)

Hearts of Gold
You all have
I derive pleasure
When advice you measure
Now
To live is treasure
Cause I'm out of pressure

I appreciate your lives
Cause it has influenced my life
In a most fabulous way
You are there when I'm down
You are there when I'm up and available for all the in betweens

You are worth more than precious stones
You have stood the test of time
And that's why I love you
Forever your Sister

29. Brother (Marvy - Only Brother)

Before a Star was born
I looked at myself feeling unfulfilled...
Something was missing
But the moment you stepped into my life
Things changed completely

My dearest brother,
My confidant
My life is more beautiful because you came right after I did
We loved...then we fought and loved some more
My life's puzzle would be incomplete without you
Because you are a good part of me
Just to remind you again just in case you ever doubt
I have loved you since you were a baby and I always will
Your Big Sis xoxo

30. KESS (Note to Self)

To be wise
Is to be quick to hear
And slow to speak

To be true
Is to say only
What you see but when necessary

To be kind
Is to be there for folks
Not when they are high alone
But also when down so low

To be good
Is to like everything positive
With negative things repulsive

To be Honest
Is to be truthful and sincere
With myself and others
Upholding integrity all the way

To be Loved
Is to Love as Christ loved
And still does,
To care deeply as He wants me to

To be Kess
Is to be myself all the time taking
One day at a time
Basking in the goodness of God

31. MY LOVE

You and You only…
You are always there for me
When I am alone or in need of company
And my life is up or down, black or white or in colours we do life together

I look to you
To chase my dark clouds away
A God sent, God's Own child
My friend, my confidant
My gist partner, my brother, my love

In the least you do
I see the most I want
Cause you are a rare stone
Which is,
Found in my yard only
And in my heart only,
You'll always be

32.   My Precious Jewels

(The 3 Es...Being your mum has been one of the best things that I have ever experienced, I love you)

Quietly,
While you were asleep
The Lord and I were talking
I asked that He always keep you warm, loved, protected...safe

He promised you the life that you do graciously and gracefully carry
You bring your light and shine into my morning
You shine so bright and effortlessly the Sun works twice as hard
Which reminds me that God is not done with you

As I think of you today and always,
In Special ways…
I know God is mindful of you, he has got your backs
As you daily warm my heart,
I asked the Lord to keep you for me
The Lord promised to hold you in the warmest embrace

And this reminds me that
You were loved before you manifested
You are loved now
You are loved always,
Phenomenally Loved

I love you. Mum ♥

33.   GOD IS

In darkness : He is your Light
When Afraid : He is your courage and strength
When Anxious : He is your Peace
When Bereaved : He is your comfort
When Defeated : He is your Victory
When Depressed : He is your Joy and Strength
When Thirsty : He is your Living water
When Doubtful : He is the Solid rock on which you stand
When Friends Fail : He sticks closer than a, brother
When Lonely : He is your company
When weary : He is your strength
When tempted : He helps you overcome

Whatever, wherever, whenever, however

He is JESUS

34. LIKE

Like a fish in a pond
I want to be
A part of your life

Like a bright light
In the darkness night
I want to be
There for you when you need me

Like your body, mind and Soul
I want to be
With you always, never leaving

Like a snail carries its shell
I want to share
Out of your ups and downs

Like a dog and it's tail
I wants us
To walk and run together
Hand in Hand

35. *Olubukolami's* Favourite Author

Bishop T. D JAKES.

My Favourite book He wrote - Let it Go: Forgive so you can be forgiven

The book sheds light on the power of forgiveness and maximising your potential in Christ through letting hurt and offenses go. Bishop T. D Jakes uses inspiration from the Lord's Prayer to show how the act of forgiving and learning to be forgiven can lead you to a more joyful, peaceful and purposeful life.

36. *Olubukolami's* Favourite Lines/Quotes

(Some witty and funny, some inspiring)

- It is a cold world, you've got to supply your own heat

- The best things in life are not seen or heard but felt by the heart - Helen Keller

- He who kneels before God can stand before anyone

- You are a student of Life, there is always something new for you to learn everyday

- Positive minds Produce positive lives

- Where there is Focus, there is Power - George Washington Carver

- Teach us to number our days that we may apply our hearts to Wisdom

- Your Mind and heart is what makes you a Winner not your Appearance or Speech - Dr Myles Munroe

- Be careful the seeds you sow today as it affects generations yet unborn, sow a good seed

- You are not rich until you have something money cannot buy

- Have Faith in God, God has Faith in you - Edwin Louis Cole

- Wherever you are in the World, you'll notice that all people smile in the same language

- Things will always get better

- A man in love schemes more than a hundred lawyers

- Love vanquishes time, to lovers a moment can be eternity, eternity can be the tick of a clock - Mary Parish

- Love doesn't make the World go round, Love is what makes the ride worthwhile - Franklin P Jones

- Love must be learned and learned again and again, there is no end to it, Hate needs no instruction but only wants to be provoked - Katherine Anne Porte

- Grow Old along with me, the best is yet to be, the last of life for which the first was made - Robert Browning

- Gratitude unlocks the fullness of life, turns a meal to a feast, a house to a home and a stranger to a friend - Olubukolami Adebayo

37. *Olubukolami's* **Favourite Colours -**
Red and Blue, recently started loving Purple

38. *Olubukolami's* Favourite Self Affirmation

Blessed and Highly Favoured (Luke 1:28)

Meaning to me - The Lord's hand is continually upon me to single me out, He looks kindly upon me, He favours me and uses me according to His will and purpose. His love for me is unconditional and unwavering. I am the chosen one, I am the Blessed one, I am special, I am the preferred one. I am the head and not the tail in all I do. Hallelujah!

39. *Olubukolami's* Favourite Holiday Destination and Holiday of the year

Favourite Holiday Destination - Paris (Capital of France)

Why? - The City oozes Love and excellence … I 'Love' Love and Excellence

Favourite Holiday of the Year - Christmas

Why? - It's the time of the year when we celebrate the Birth of our Lord Jesus Christ, who was born to die for our sins so we can be reconciled to the Father

Secondly, it's a time of love, family and friends, sharing and caring, lovely feasts and gift giving. I also love the decorations and decorating, I have always loved Christmas time since I was a little girl,It's a love I won't outgrow. Simply love Christmas time.

40. *Olubukolami's* Testimony

40 Years of God's Faithfulness

I want to thank God for His Faithfulness in my life for the past four decades, I can boldly say God has been good to me in every area of my life. It has been 100% Him and no one else.

I thank God for the impeccable health I have enjoyed for the last 40 years, I have never been admitted to the hospital for any other reason apart from giving birth to our 3 beautiful children. I thank God for the covenant of health.

I thank God for the gift of a nuclear and extended family, for the family of God and for lasting friendships and meaningful relationships.

I thank God for success in all I do and most of all for the gift of life, I do not take this for granted. I am eternally be grateful to God

I pray that the Lord that has kept me thus far will continue to keep me for the next 40 years and beyond if He tarries in Jesus name (Amen)

Printed in the United States
by Baker & Taylor Publisher Services